My Life in a Changing World

Douglas Morris

First Published November 2024
Imprint: Independently published

© Douglas Morris

The rights of Douglas Morris to be identified as the author of this work has been assessed in accordance with the Copyright, Designs and Patent Act 1988.

All rights reserved including moral rights.

No parts of this book may be reprinted or reproduced or utilised in any form or by any electronic, mechanical or other means, now known, or hereafter invented, including photocopying and recording, or in any information, storage or retrieval system, without permission in writing from the Author.

Contents

1. Family background   5
2. Our house   9
3. Growing up   12
4. War years   17
5. School years   19
6. National service   23
7. Starting work   25
8. Marriage and home   27
9. Career   32
10. Family life   33
11. Retirement   35

12.	Changes over my lifetime	38
13.	Some things have gone	42
14.	There are more of some things!	46

1. Family background

I was born on the 2 August 1931 at 4 North Gardens Merton, SW19, and brought up by my parents, Henry Cecil Morris and Lilian Maude Marie (nee Parfett). I might have had an older Brother, Cecil, born 08.01.28 but he died of pneumonia 3 November 1929. My Mother once told me that I also had a poor start to life as I started out with a leaking heart valve and was raised on Goats' milk. My three younger Sisters were all born there; Joan (12 February 1935), Phyllis (11 August 1936) and Hazel (16 June 1939).

My father's ancestry may have hailed from the London and Southwark area. He was a builder and decorator, although why he chose this profession is a mystery because he performed well in the Civil Service Exam which would have been a respectable and well paid career in those days. During the second world war served as an ARP (Air Raid Precaution) Warden. He was though held back from full armed service and employed instead on building the Mulberry Docks in Surrey Quays. These were huge, floating concrete harbours which were towed across the English Channel to provide a sea borne base for ships attending the Normandy invasions. He also worked on airstrips in the West Country. The latter affected his health from which he never fully recovered.

My mothers' family were descended from 'Perfects', Blackies and Goldings possibly from Scotland and London with several addresses in St Giles, Whitechapel and many references to workhouses. Before marriage my mother was in service and was an accomplished machinist. She also played the piano, and had an old style piano which had adjustable candle holders.

I was only aware of one grandparent, which was my mother's mother. Emily Parfett, whose husband served as a bandsman in the Irish Guards, lived in an Alms House in Garrett Lane, Tooting with three sons (Walter, Jimmy and Ernest) and two daughters (Lillian and Helen). Walter suffered breathing problems affected it would appear working in the boiler rooms at St George's Hospital. Jimmy was an accomplished woodworker/joiner who emigrated to Australia but returned after many years. On a train journey he was struck by a brick thrown at the window. Helen worked in confectionary modelling cake icing decoration. Ernest served in the Kings Own Scottish Borderers as a bandsman and batman. He spent many years in India, stationed near the

Khyber pass, where pastimes included strong tea, hockey and building stage sets. In the war he was in action in France and sustained a stomach injury in the tank battle around the 1944 battle for Caen. 'Uncle Ernie' would be a regular contact throughout my life.

2. Our house

Colliers Wood is midway between Tooting Broadway and South Wimbledon, all being tube stations on the Northern Line. The High Street was also served by Trams with the track in the centre of the road; with power from a middle channel (Seats were reversible depending on the direction of travel) it contained a number of small shops and a pub on the one side with a large Co-op on the other side. Tin tokens were given as a credit for purchases and exchanged for cash when a dividend was declared. Next to the Co-op was a Garage, behind which was the 2nd Mitcham Scout Hall in Park Road, and on the corner was fish/chip shop. Street deliveries included the ice cream man with Walls ice lollies and the cats' meat man. Their vehicles were three wheeled bicycles with a cool box.

North Gardens and South Gardens were connected by Valley Gardens, having been developed in the early 1900's to the rear of Colliers Wood Underground Station. The three roads formed an H, Valley Gardens connecting the other two roads. I grew up in 4 North Gardens which was an end of terrace of four houses, two situated in North Gardens and the other two in Valley Gardens.

Number 4, being on a bend, had a large front garden, large garage and a small triangular rear garden. It faced down to the High Street giving a view of the passing Trams. The house comprised a dining room, front room, scullery downstairs and upstairs two large bedrooms, a box bedroom and bathroom/toilet. The living rooms/main bedrooms each had a fireplace installed which was the means of heating. Coal for the fires was delivered by Webb the Coalman, with a horse drawn cart. He would carry the sacks though the house for those without a side entrance. During the war I collected in an old pram our ration of coke from the Gas Works in Western Road. Before "smokeless zones" were legislated. London and large Cities suffered from Smog (combination of Fog, smoke and fumes). The drains in the street were also regularly flushed and rubbish in all forms placed in a galvanised dustbin which was also collected

The Scullery contained a built in Larder (no refrigerator) and a laundry mangle (large wooden rollers turned by hand (rubber buttons survived but many shirts finished up with a few half pearl buttons). Clothes were washed by hand in the stone sink. Hot water was provided by a back boiler to the living room fire. In the early years baths were taken in a tin bath in front of the fire, water was heated in saucepans on the gas stove. Later a gas boiler was installed in the Bathroom which lit up with a loud bang each time.

Our next door neighbours were Mr and Mrs Cruft, and Mr Cruft was a highly accomplished Double Bass player in a London Orchestra. On the other side lived the Barringers with a Daughter the age of Phyllis and a younger Son John. Mr Barringer owned and ran a Newsagent/Sweet Shop next door the Merton Bus Garage. A couple of years ago, in the 2000's, John made contact some 70 years after we played together, and we have since kept in touch. He drove us Down to Emsworth to visit Harry Taylor, another old neighbour.

3. Growing up

On one side of North Gardens were the Singlegate Infants and Senior Schools. My prized possession was a peddle car, probably because I had few other toys, and as an inducement on the first day of school I was allowed to ride my pedal car to School.

I can remember the first song I learnt, "Oh I do like to be beside the seaside....". My Teacher for three years was Miss Wood who was well liked by the class. We learned the Alphabet from pictures the teacher had drawn. She dispensed Cod Liver Oil & Malt to some of the class including myself. The jars were kept in the fireplace and hidden by a screen. On fine days lessons were held in the small garden which faced Church Road. I have memories of the seemingly very tall Foxgloves.

Both South and North Gardens provided an entrance to a recreation ground, containing football pitch, gardens, band stand and play area. In my early years I played a lot within the three streets and the recreation ground. Only a few houses had a garage and rarely was a car seen in any of the three roads so that the roads were safe to play in. Games of marbles were held in the gutter and the drains had to be avoided. A wicket was chalked on a lampost or telegraph pole and, unless a bat was available, scoring was means of kicking a tennis ball. The object of the game of "bad eggs" was to hit a moving player with a tennis ball. Whilst cars were rare, my father did own an Austin 7, and I recall holidays at a campsite in Whitstable and at the Harrietsham smallholding of the Lee family who were kinfolk. The latter journey involved my father driving the Austin up a steep hill whilst we walked alongside.

I joined the 2nd Mitcham Cubs who met in a dusty hall opposite Wandle Park. It was lit by gas, invariably with a mantle or two missing. I recall enjoying a game called "Mowgli I'm King of the Jungle". I followed on by joining the Scout Troop which held two meetings a week in a hall it owned in Park Road which included a large hall with a stage and a room for each of the Patrols. The first meeting was for Scouting matters and the second for games; Handball, Hop the Barger, and Band practise. I played a bugle, performing once a month for Church Parade. I ended up as a Patrol Leader but could not gain the King Scout Badge as I was not a swimmer.

Annual Scout Camps were held under tents on Cathanger Farm near Petworth. Latrines were of a primitive nature. Ground sheets and blankets formed the bedding. I remember my time in the Scouts with fond memories and found it character building. Happy memories of camping as a Group. Scout Camp at Frylands I made the evening chocolate drink in a Dixie containing Prunes which were soaking overnight. The examiner was impressed with the taste.

In a select team in the District Camping Competition, held in Frylands, Featherbed Lane, we won in 1946. Inadvertently, I prepared the evening soup (Symington cubes) in the Dixie containing prunes in soak. The examiner was impressed with taste. There were other District sporting competitions and Church Parades. In 1945 we entered a football team in a local league, Croydon & District, and came first. I left Scouts when the Family moved to Wallington.

I moved on to the Senior School for a year, where my Teacher was "Topsy" Turner. He was keen on arithmetic and each week he held a mental arithmetic test, which I found to my liking. He coached cricket and practises were held in the playground on an asphalt wicket with the stumps in a wooden stand, although I did not impress him with my batting!

4. War years

When the Second World War started in September 1939 I was attending the senior school and was evacuated by the school for a short time to Ludgershall, near Midhurst. My Mother and three sisters stayed with Lord and Lady Walker near Billingshurst, but in the servants' quarters. During a lull I returned home but was soon sent away again. This time on my own to Uton, near Crediton Devon. I was billeted with Mr and Mrs King and their two sons, Anthony and Ivan. Mr King was a shepherd for the nearby farmer. Although Mr and Mrs King were very nice people, I found the experience stressful, and I was bullied by their elder son, causing nervousness and frequent bedwetting.

During the occasions I returned home I would help my father on his allotment, the football pitch at the end of the road having been turned over to allotments. My father worked his allotment well and it was productive. Horse droppings in the road were much sought after for composting. I used to walk to Guttridges in South Wimbledon to buy seeds. The seeds were weighed in ounces, poured into small brown envelopes with hand written details.

After my return, I overcame bed wetting by sleeping on a sheet of mahogany. I also gained entrance to Mitcham Grammar School for Boys in 1942 but in 1944 I was again evacuated, also on my own. This time I went to Lincoln where I attended the City School for Boys. I first stayed with Mr and Mrs Issott at their Smallholding in Skellingthorpe and subsequently with Mr and Mrs Buckthorpe, daughter Joan and son Freddie, both older than me, at 263 Newark Road, Bracebridge. There were two airfields close by, the flight path for one flew over the smallholding at Skellingthorpe and I witnessed returning Lancasters Bombers shot up and feathered propellers. Whilst at Bracebridge there was a loud bang, the windows rattled and we could see debris flying on the skyline, when a bomber crashed on landing.

5. School years

The experience of evacuation was disruptive to many families and evacuees. Evacuation held back progress in my education and I could not catch up with French and Latin. My abiding thought is that I cannot remember saying farewell to any of the Host family or keeping in touch. I suppose the legacy of evacuation was I took all changes as a matter of fact which took a while to overcome in later life and now hold friendships dearly. I returned to Colliers Wood for good in 1945 and was able to renew friendships with my pals in the vicinity and the Scouts. Scouting was helpful in getting back on my feet.

I was interviewed by the Head Master, A.J.Doig, for a place at the Grammar School in Mitcham. The Grammar School was equally character building, with the emphasis on learning and engaging in sport, singing and acting. School dinners were nourishing but bland We were supplied each day with a third of a pint bottle of milk in a stubby bottle with a cardboard cap. The teachers, mainly men, were first class but unfortunately I wasted the academic opportunities but seem to retain sufficient knowledge for my business career.

I produced our play, Hewers of Coal, in the School House Competition. Set in the Mine which had collapsed. This was created by coal being dropped from over the back screen. Stage Master was not impressed. During the performance the battery operated lamp was due to dim and luckily did flicker on time. In a School rugby match at Bec School I was sent off by the Master refereeing who overheard my remark on his decisions. Our accompanying Master was however in agreement with me and our Head Master took no action.

I formed a number of close chums and their families Don Carter, Bill Everett and Derek Kinsley, often staying overnight. Annual Harvest Camps were held under Tents in a field behind Midhurst Ruins. We were paid a penny a mile if we cycled and our kit was taken by train from Mitcham Station. We were sent out to local farms to help in various ways for which we received a modest payment. I worked in various places; weeding in the vegetable garden of the Cowdray Estate, picking dwarf beans in an experimental garden centre at Fernhurst, picking up potatoes and helping in corn fields. On a different occasion Don Carter and I cycled to Harrietsham (which is past Maidstone) for a week of strawberry picking. My Uncle Henry Lee, Aunt Ethel (Dad's sister), older cousins Eddie, David and Donald (about my age) worked a smallholding there before emigrating to Hamilton, New Zealand. During my last school summer holiday I worked at Sandals Wood Yard in Ross Road, Wallington.

The North Gardens house was sold for £2,500 on 3 August 1949 and on 4th August we moved to 23 Beddington Gardens, Wallington (PP £4,200). This was a large, red brick residence, formerly a doctor's home and Surgery, with a large garden including a pond and air raid shelter over which flew planes to and from Croydon Airport (Britain's first, true passenger airport). The family occupied two large living rooms and four bedrooms and my father converted some of the rooms to provide two Flats and two Flatlets. I kept up my schooling in Mitcham which required a long cycle every day from Wallington to Mitcham, often cycling home late after rugby training (and later pub visits).

6. National Service

Upon leaving school I was due for National Service but entry was delayed whilst I awaited an opportunity for aircrew. Eventually I failed the medical on account of a weak right eye. During the wait I worked at Marks & Spencer, Tooting Broadway as stock room assistance with my Uncle John. I also worked, with two OM's ('Old Mitchamian' rugby), Brian Mitchell and Tony North, as a table clearer at the ABC Restaurant which was set up in Battersea Park as part of the Festival of Britain in 1951. As part of Mitcham's Festival week, the Old Mitchamians took part in a 7-a-side tournament at the Mitcham Stadium on July 14th.

In February 1952 I commenced National Service at Padgate for enrolment and kit. A week later sent for "Square Bashing" at RAF Weeton, Blackpool Tower could be seen from the parade ground. A rigid routine including moving within the hut on squares of blanket. Whilst there, another disappointment, as I failed an interview to become an Officer Cadet. Then on to Hereford for trade training as a Progress

Clerk and taught to touch type, after which a permanent posting to RAF Bircham Newton, near Kings Lynn, established as a School of Administration. The first person I met was a classmate from school, Don Donovan.

My duties were to type the reports made on Flying Officers posted on a course to update administration knowledge. The reports were typed as one plus four carbon copies. No rubbing out was allowed so my touch typing reverted two fingers. I shared a Billet with Don Donovan, Jeff Masters, Tony Simmonds. We, together with Eric Chapman, were members of the Station Rugby fifteen and Cricket Eleven. Eric ran the Station pig farm, curious as pigs do not fly. With our help Jeff ran the Tombola sessions, the profit providing for a meal in Kings Lynn.

During my stay the Wing Commander took me up in a Tiger Moth (including a Loop) and a Meteor trainer (including handling the controls) which was exhilarating flights. Whilst I was Duty Clerk one evening Prince Phillip came into land as a trainee Pilot, during a snow storm. A Royal Residence was nearby at Sandringham.

7. Starting work

My National Service was completed in February 1954, leaving as a Senior Aircraftman 2546803. Barry Pritchard (OM Club Captain) recommended me to the Northern Assurance Co., which I joined in March 1954 as a clerk in the Accounts Department, located in the Head Office at 1 Moorgate opposite the bank of England. The starting salary was £24.7s. 3d, but it was very boring work. Assurance Companies and Banks were regarded as jobs for life. Starting salaries were low as were increments. Promotion was usually in "dead man's shoes".

I was however fortunate to transfer into the Mortgage Department the following year, where I first met up with Bill Evans, a Senior Clerk, although in those days transferring from departments or joining other Companies was frowned upon and would be treated as being a "rolling stone". The advantages were a sound Pension Scheme and a generous House Purchase funding (men only!).

There were opportunities for sport, drama and social events, and time off was allowed for sporting events. I played in both the office rugby team (including five other OM's – Barry, Brian Ives, Brian Goldney, Tony Gathercole and Brain Bolton) and the Combined Insurance Offices as well as the Athletic team. We played with and against International Rugby Stars. As a rugby player I was a centre three quarter (15's) and flyhalf (7's). Derek Kinsley was my partner in the centre and Don Carter was scrumhalf. Brian Goldney was fullback. Tony Gathercole joined the Harlequins, playing on the wing.

8. Marriage & home

I met Marjorie Chave when she worked for the White Cross Insurance Company which was a subsidiary of the Northern. She was a keen netball player in the Office team. We married on 2nd August 1958. Marjorie and I first lived in an upstairs Flat at 26 Thornhill Gardens, West Croydon but we bought 11 South Walk on the 12th July 1959 for £3,150 (now valued around £600,000). Catalpa trees lined the road and no cars were parked anywhere. Milk was delivered daily. Coal /Coke was delivered at intervals. Next door at No. 13 Lived an elderly blind lady (Mrs Crawford) who would light her fires and spread the ashes on her driveway.

Subsequent, improvements made were Central Heating, side and rear extension, double glazing and crazy paving driveway/patio. Taking after my Father I painted, wallpapered, wall lights, coving and built cupboards. I cultivated vegetable patches at the end of the garden, and continued to garden throughout my life. I planted the Bramley apple tree on 05/11/66 (½ standard – cost 25 shillings).

I scrubbed Westoby's the Bakers bakehouse floor (blobs of dough stuck to the concrete floor) in order to pay for feeding our first dog, an Alsation – Rusty. Later we had a Labrador - Christie and then another Alsation – Kimberly. Other pets include two white Doves - Abelard and Eloise, a rabbit, a Canary and a Goldfish.

I turned to Football after being married, playing in the Office 2nd XL. Once scored a hat trick, left and right foot and a header. Best position was an overlapping right back. Home fixtures were at New Beckenham enabling me to use my rail season ticket and keeping the cost down. Sent off once for continuous dissent, although wrongly identified, was banned for seven days.

9. Career

On the 8th of April 1968 the Northern Head Office was relocated to Knollys House, beside East Croydon Station. On the 15 July 1968 we moved to the Commercial Union building in Leadenhall Street, the Northern having just been taken over by the Commercial Union. Despite the unsatisfactory working arrangements, I revived the rugby team during my brief stay.

On 14 July 1969 I joined the Mortgage Department of the Friends Provident & Century Insurance Co., Leadenhall Street. The Office was formed by Quakers in 1832 in Bradford. I was understudy to the Joint Mortgage Managers and was appointed Manager upon their retirement. The building was sold and the department was relocated on the 20 October 1975 to the Dorking premises in Pixham Lane. The Mortgage department merged with the Property Department with Bill Evans as Estates Department Manager.

The General Manager at Friends Provident was presenting an important Speech to all Departmental Managers at Dorking. I arranged to pick up a City Manager who lived in South Croydon. About to pull up outside his house when the brake pedal went through the floor. He went by train and arrived in a pick-up truck. Entered the hall moaning about the quality of Office cars. In fact it was mine originally and bought by the Office at the time Managers were being provided with a car.

Jim Wallis and I devised and took part in skits for the Sports & Social Club Shows. When the Bar Staff were on holiday we ran it, making a profit on sandwiches. I helped organise the Office Fetes. On 2nd August 1981 a new sports centre was opened and County players marked the centre's opening. I played in the Office Squash leagues but my enjoyment of Badminton took off, playing for the Office in the local leagues. I Played in a mixed match against the Bank of England and my partner was a junior county player, who took command of our partnership with many subsequent anecdotes. The FP Mens Badminton played a Dorking Town team at a Hall situated over shops in Dorking High Street. There were two hazards, being the close proximity to the side line of an old style rectangular fireguard and the fact that the floor had been generously polished. I had persuaded a senior member of management to play and was in fear he would slip and injure himself. Embarrassment on the badminton court during mixed doubles! Playing to the gallery I pretended to slap my partner on the bottom. Unfortunately she stepped back onto my hand, much to the amusement of the spectators. Seen on TV during FP Sponsored Badminton Tournament at the Albert Hall, in an interview with a reporter before entering Wembley Conference Centre, at an Any Questions programme held near London Bridge.

Jim Wallis and I joined the Office Football Team on tours to Belgium as the "Elder Statesmen". Traditionally, all had to wear a fancy hat after breakfast until evening meal. Mine was a chefs hat and Jim's was a Fez although I was permitted to Referee without mine!

10. Family life

Jacqueline was born on 7 August 1959 and Richard on 25 October 1962. Our house was always busy. Uncle Ernie stayed with us on a number of weekends helping with odd jobs. During the year he would purchase a considerable number of items and at Christmas these would be wrapped and numbered and attached to a trellis positioned in the lounge. Family and visiting friends would draw a raffle ticket and locate the prize. On Guy Fawkes night we would build. a bonfire in the garden and let off fireworks. We shared the event with the Honour family who backed on to the end fence and a gateway was installed in the fence for easy access.

Cars were always important to get around for work and outings. We started with a pale blue Triumph Herald, but other cars included my parents old Austin A40, an Austin Maxi, Mini Metro, Volkswagen Golf, and Nissans. Some months after Jury Service I was questioned by the Police in the case of a murder, the body of a prostitute had been found on Epsom Downs. She frequented the Clapham Common area where my car had been seen one evening. It was some weeks later that I recalled, with great relief, the car had that evening been in a South Croydon Garage and collected the following day!

For many years we drove to Clacton and stayed in caravans there for our annual holiday, taking Marjorie's mum with us. Later, we flew with Dan Air and new package holidays to Spain, and America. We also sometimes travelled with our friends the Schofields who had moved away from West Wickham to the New Forest, and we often stayed with them or they with us. Succeeding occupants next door at No. 13 were the Cooks, Burchetts and currently the Smallridges (Jeff, Maureen and Lindsay, Nichola and Georgina) with whom we became very good friends since they moved in during August 1984. In recent years Jeff has become a close friend and been helpful to me on many occasions. We also made friends with Don/Shirley Thomas at 17 S.W. and spent holidays abroad with them. Don and I were once thought to be brothers.

Finally, hobbies and of course sport were important to me. I played Badminton, dabbled with rugby, got involved in the set up and running of Coney Hall Football Club. I helped to run the West Wickhm

Operatic Society and acted on regular occasions. In the WWOS production of Fiddler on the Roof another cast member and myself forgot to wheel on the piano, leaving the pianist pretending to play. She has since forgiven us.

11. Retirement

I officially retired from work on July 1992 but carried on for another two years as a Consultant. What followed was weekly spells behind the counter of Richard's Shop (a bit like Arkright in "open all hours"), The Toffee Tin in Waterloo Street, Brighton/Hove. It was the typical convenient stores with a cross section of customers – on one occasion the boxer Chris Eubank. Separately, Marjorie and I helped run the shop, sometimes passing one another on the M23. During one of these occasions No 11 was burgled and jewellery stolen, after which an Alarm System was installed. The shop never really paid its way although the residential accommodation was value for the rent.

When the shop had gone, opportunities were taken to embark on walking and golfing holidays, membership of HF Holidays, National Trust, Way & Arun Canal Trust and Windmill section of SPAB (The Society for the Protection of Ancient Buildings).

Doug Morris, Dougie James, Derek Kinsley
Rugby mates for 70 years

After my parents had died, our old family house in Mitcham was sold off by myself and a Solicitor, acting as Administrators, on 25.01.88 for £910,000, out of which a house was bought for Mrs Hazel Brown (nee Morris) for £150,000 at 11 Smitham Bottom Lane, Purley. The Will created a family issue in that it was biased in favour of Hazel who inherited the house and sale proceeds The Will also contained a bequest of £100,000 to her divorced husband. There was a suspicion of a covert action in that Mrs Brown lived at home and tended my mother. No mention was made to me in arranging a will, although I was a frequent visitor. On two occasions I stayed overnight to allow Mr and Mrs Brown a holiday. Mrs Brown was approached by Mrs Corlett to review terms of the Will but this was declined. Mrs Phyllis Corlett (nee Morris) prepared a file but could not obtain Legal Aid although divorced and penniless. The case came before a Judge in Chambers at the Law Courts where Mrs Joan Murray (nee Morris) was represented by Scottish Solicitors and awarded £100,000. In her absence I put the case for Mrs Corlett but was unsuccessful. At the time the Will was made no account was made of the fact the Mrs Murray was a Widow with three Daughters and limited means and Mrs Corlett was Divorced in South Africa without means of provision, moving to the Isle Man and dependant on her three Sons.

12. Changes over my lifetime

Socks with holes are now thrown away and not darned. Shirts are frequently worn outside trousers and not tucked (I wore detachable collar and cuffs to the shirt when I started work). Shoes were repaired with stick on rubber soles. Football boots had nail on leather studs. The football had leather panels with a laced up opening and an inner bladder. Refuse collection has changed with emphasis on recycling materials and bins are placed at the front of the property. Newspapers are no longer used for wrapping Fish & Chips and as toilet sheets during world war two. Many items of food and fruit are pre wrapped.

Smokeless zones have been set up with the result coal fires are no longer in use. Home heating is generally carried out by a Gas Fired Boiler, electrically supplied radiators. A few have converted to wood burning stoves. The weather patterns have altered and are not as predictably seasonal. The causes of climate change due to fossil fuels and other forms of pollution are being explored.

Sunday used to be a day of rest with little activity taking place, but most shops are open for business. High Street shopping has changed with many being occupied by Coffee Shops and Charity Shops. Shopping Centres, with large name stores providing the attraction, are in the most Towns and Cities.

Some County Towns, including Bromley, have been incorporated into a "London Borough" and London Boroughs have taken over the former independent Townships (Beckenham, Orpington and West Wickham are now part of and controlled by Bromley). Local taxation has changed from a Rateable Value of property to the Market Value of property, which is subject to periodic review. The original train formations (GWR, LMS, LNER and SR) were Nationalised and more recently broken up into Franchised Regions. However, Trams are returning in some towns.

The traditional Business scenario of ownership and independence has changed with mergers, takeovers and Financial groups (Private Equity). Ownership has also been acquired by foreign interests. The traditional Business scenario of ownership and independence has changed with mergers, takeovers and Financial Groups (Northern Assurance taken over by Commercial Union in turn taken over by Norwich Union, now Aviva). Friends Provident taken over by Resolution, renamed Friends Life, and recently acquired by Aviva. Ownership of Property and Businesses has been acquired by Private Equity Groups and Foreign firms seeking a profit. There are many Betting Shops and Lotteries (National and Health).

Currency/Measurement (Linear and Liquid) is now based on the metric units of ten. 100 pence to the Pound instead of 240. A Yard of 36 inches has given way to a Meter of 100 Centimetres (approximately 39and ½ inches). Liquid measurement of Pints/Quarts has given way to Litres. Recognition of Gay and Lesbian relationships, with the legality of marriages. Buses do not have a Conductor giving tickets with the name of the stops on the route but now show the destination electronically. More recently the fare is by card current/credit or prepaid card (Oyster).

Academic Schooling has changed from Secondary (basic teaching) and Grammar (academic) to Comprehensive Schools for all abilities. Polytechnics have been raised to University status. Fees for a University place are repaid following obtaining employment. Companies are offering fees paid University placements.

Some things have however stayed the same! Time remains a 24 hour clock and the Months of the Year and number of days has stayed unaltered!

13. Some things are gone

My old house at Wallington has gone, and replaced with retirement flats.

In the gardens of my old house in Willington

On a recent visit to the City of Lincoln I went back to the areas where I had been evacuated during the war. I found the house in Skellingthorpe burnt down and the house in Bracebridge demolished to make way for the extension to the adjacent Walkers Crisp Factory (Smiths in my day). The Scout Hut which helped me to re-acclimatise after evacuation has gone for development and the Scout Group no longer exists (what happened to the band instruments?).

The School is now a Catholic Middle School. The News of the World sports ground (where the School used the athletic track and the opportunity for an OM –Brian Hewson- to run in the Olympics) is an open area and the large house converted to a Pub/Restaurant. The Old Mitchamians Rugby Club ceased in 1969 and converted to an open club, Mitcham RUFC. (now Mitcham & Carshalton RUFC), which has a club house and pitches in Poulter Park, Mitcham. On the adjoining ground is Tooting & Mitcham Football Club. The School playing field, next to Mitcham Station, is now a Recreation ground. The Mitcham Stadium where I played was replaced with a housing estate. The lavender fields that were once a large part of the area have all but disappeared, save for a small farm over towards Woodmansterne.

There are no trams operating in Colliers Wood High Street. Trolley Buses have been taken out of service, they used to travel through Tooting, Mitcham and Croydon. Croydon Airport no longer operates, with most of the land developed for housing, school and leisure. Croydon Airport has long since been closed down for flying and is now a Museum and the airfield area redeveloped. Smaller "Battle of Britain" airfields (Biggin Hill, Kenley etc.) are limited to private flying.

The Postal service has been reduced due to the rise in the use the Computer (E-Mail, Facebook etc) and Mobile Phones. Public Houses have reduced in numbers and those remaining combine conventional service with a catering facility. Woolworths, the original "pound shop" ceased trading after many years as also has C&A's.

The "Fear Factor" no longer exists despite Legislation (disposing of litter – using mobile phones when driving – increase in crime). Etiquette/Discipline has deteriorated (queueing at a busy bus stop is disorganised). Organised gatherings supporting a cause, dubious or otherwise. have increased. Health and Safety, Political Correctness, Traffic restrictions all contribute to restrain the freedom of activity and speech that existed in my early years.

Despite all the changes that have taken place there is still a purposeful nostalgic activity. The preservation of properties of historic interest by bodies such as the National Trust (e.g. Chartwell) and re-opening disused railways (e g Bluebell Railway). There is also the Society for the Protection of Ancient Buildings (e.g. Windmills). The preservation of waterways (e.g. Wey & Arun Canal trust). There are societies endeavouring to protect Fauna, Flora and Wildlife. There are many charitable societies for worthy causes (e.g. British Red Cross and the British Legion).

14. There are more of some things

Whereas only one house in South, North and Valley Gardens had a TV, every house has at least one. Most houses now have double glazing. Cameras have developed considerably since the old black and white Box Camera. Cars have increased in number and few are parked in a garage. Charity collections have increased since the Poppy Day collection. Landline phones can be placed in rooms around the house and can operate at some distance. Electronics has advanced in such as Security, Catering etc. Space Exploration with the advent of a Rocket to the Moon.

There now many opportunities to participate in an increased number of sporting/social activities and within which coaching is available. There are also large out of Town shopping estates (B&Q, Asda, Makro, Wicks, Ikea, Bluewater etc). These latter developments have increased the traffic flow. Street lights of Lanterns upon upright iron posts have been replaced with Concrete posts and overhanging Halogen Lights.

Motorways have been constructed to improve transport travel for both private and commercial transport. The M25 ring road (a radius of between 13/22 miles) around Greater London was completed in 1986 and is 117 miles (188km) long. Travel by Aircraft has increased enormously and major towns have an Airport .

Electronics has improved many areas such as Security, Catering etc. The means of photography has increased. Apart from the improvement of the conventional camera, mobile phones incorporate the facility. Photographs can be transmitted by Computer. Communications have progressed rapidly since the early days of BBC Television with the introduction of Commercial TV, Mobile Phones, I-Pads and the launching of Satellites circling the earth. Who could have thought a Rocket to the Moon was to occur, with personnel aboard. Restaurants were for the few, pubs only sold beer and spirits, but now there is a proliferation of eateries, including at pubs.

A considerable change in clothing. Women chose to wear what was formerly menswear, such as trousers and hats. A large increase in single parents and the divorce rate. In recent times there has been a considerable increase in the population with other nationalities and as a consequence many formal notifications are printed in other languages.

The range of medicines has increased as also the identities and cure of diseases. Life expectancy has gone up, but the population is now ageing and less fit.

What changes I have seen!

Thank you for reading my story.

Douglas Morris

Footnotes

1: A broader picture of events and the nature of changes and how these were brought about is to be found in "A History of Modern Britain" (ISBN 978-0-330-43983-1) by Andrew Marr.

2: The circumstance involving evacuation and how the disruption and experience affected families and evacuees can be read in "When the Children came Home" (ISBN 978-1-84739) by Julie Summers.

3: Growing up in the 1930s. Read " A 1930s Childhood " (ISBN 978 0 7509 9724 9).

Printed in Great Britain
by Amazon